LILLENAS DRAMA

THIS IS YOUR LIFE

by Jan Peterson Ewen

Lillenas PUBLISHING COMPANY
KANSAS CITY, MO 64141

Dedication

It is my great privilege to dedicate this book to the loves of my life—
my son, Peter; my daughters, Rebecca and Rachel;
and my incredibly gifted husband and faithful friend,
Bruce. My life is richly blessed.

Contents

Introduction

There are two areas of my life that require enormous energy and produce immeasurable joy—my family and the theatre. During our last production, a devoted young participant remarked to my youngest daughter, "I wish my mom was a director." To which my six-year-old responded, "Oh no you don't! When your mom's the director, your costume is the last one done and you're always the last ones to leave the church."

Drama consumes, supports, encourages, exposes, teaches, and develops us. We pick up the script as we are and put it down as we will become. Hearts are touched, tears are shed, and laughter is shared. We tell the stories of life and create new stories through the telling. If you have yet to be involved in a theatrical venture, you may assume I am romanticizing or exaggerating. If you have experienced the world of dramatic presentation, you know what I mean.

I share these thoughts to encourage you to work hard, be faithful, persevere, love each other through it all, and you will be amazed how God will bless your efforts—great or small. Remember, God is the Master storyteller.

The hand of God is strongly felt in our drama ministry. I have not experienced relationship building opportunities more effective than working together on a theatrical presentation. Theater provides such a wide variety of ways to plug people in. It is a comfortable way to make the church accessible to members of the community and provide a "port of entry."

Drama in worship adds that visual element that helps us process information. We're all aware of the old adage—a picture's worth a thousand words. Pictures create emotions, and emotions affect our attitudes, actions, and decisions. Introducing short, illustrative dramas in worship will bring new life to your services and new opportunities to your congregation. God bless you in all you do.

Dig Deep

Theme: All We Have to Give/The Widow's Offering

Scripture: Mark 12:38-44

Synopsis: In the scripture passage from Mark, Jesus is observing the wealthy as they lavishly give a small portion of their riches to the Temple. The widow, on the other hand, gives quietly out of her poverty—all she has to live on. In the drama "Dig Deep," Tyler gives a minuscule donation to a less fortunate person, all the time flaunting his wealth and opportunity. But the greater gift comes when the street person returns the donation so that Tyler will have change for the bus fare. Jesus indicates that it is the portion we give that is the true mark of generosity and the purity of heart with which we offer our gift that aligns us with God's will. It is this trust in God's constant care and abundance, coupled with our willingness to extend all we have in service to God into the world, that blesses us and blesses the gifts we offer.

Cast:
TYLER*
DENNIS*
PASSERS-BY
*Not gender specific

Props:
Old guitar case
Harmonica
Briefcase
Coins
Sign: "Bus Stop"
Sign: "Thanks for helping"

Setting: A bus stop on a downtown street

(A street person, DENNIS, *enters. He [she] is wearing tattered clothing and looks very unkempt. He shuffles in, carrying an old guitar case and carefully situates himself on the ground near the bus stop sign. Methodically he opens the guitar case and takes out a harmonica and a handmade sign with the words "Thanks for helping." He leans the sign against the case and starts to play the harmonica. Several well-dressed* PASSERS-BY *enter, hear* DENNIS *playing his harmonica, and drop coins into the case. Another person ignores him and scoots past. Finally,* TYLER *enters dressed in a nice suit and carrying a briefcase. He crosses to the bus stop. He has never ridden on public transportation before and is unsure what to do.* TYLER *notices* DENNIS *playing his harmonica.)*

TYLER *(to* DENNIS*):* I am assuming that the public transit picks up passengers daily at this coordinate and offers transport to the business district.

DENNIS *(stops playing, hesitates):* Yeah, the bus stops here. *(Plays harmonica)*

TYLER *(checking watch; uncomfortable):* Does this public passenger vehicle meet its scheduled rounds at reliable intervals?

DENNIS *(stops playing):* Yeah, it's usually on time.

TYLER: Good, good. I'm not accustomed to public transportation.

DENNIS: No kidding?

TYLER: Actually, I've avoided public forms of transportation all my life. Those worn-out, sticky seats sat upon by the frightening, cacophonous, writhing sea of humanity. *(Shivers, gives* DENNIS *a critical look; lightens up)* But, unfortunately, today I'm stuck.

DENNIS *(hesitating):* Well, we can all expect to have a bad day now and then. Murphy's Law.

TYLER: Isn't that the truth. I took my BMW in for its 5,000 mile check-up yesterday and, can you believe it, the garage couldn't get it done until this evening!

DENNIS: Disgraceful. You'd think a Beemer would get you instant respect in a society like this. What's the world coming to when you drive an expensive foreign car and you're still treated like a commoner! *(Plays harmonica)*

TYLER: Exactly! *(Noticing sign, takes coins from pocket and drops into guitar case)* Here you go. Coffee's on me.

DENNIS *(flatly):* Thank you for your unparalleled generosity.

TYLER: Oh, no problem. Glad to contribute. *(Sighs)* Ah, it does feel good to help those less fortunate than yourself. *(Fearing he's said the wrong thing)* Not that you're all that *un*fortunate or anything, but . . . well, you could use a new coat and . . . I'll be truthful—a bath wouldn't hurt either.

DENNIS: Yeah, well, my gold card's maxed out.

TYLER: Oh, how well I know that scenario. *(Pause)* I'd give you more cash to help out, but I've already reached my limit on tax-deductible contributions for the year.

DENNIS: Don't lose sleep over it, pal. I'm sure you gave all you could.

TYLER: Oh, I did. Absolutely. I'm stretched to the limit.

DENNIS: You look it. *(Looking for bus)* Here comes the downtown bus. Right on time. *(Closes guitar case; stands)*

TYLER: Oh . . . you're riding this bus too?

DENNIS *(shrugs):* Gotta make a livin'. I go where the action is. I guess you could say I'm a commuter too. You better get your fare ready. These bus riders can eat a straggler alive. They get vicious. If you don't keep that line movin', your life won't be worth squat.

TYLER: Oh, my fare. *(Searching pockets for money)* Uh, I must have some change somewhere . . . *(Continues to search)* Well, this is ridiculous. I stopped at the ATM on my way home last night . . .

DENNIS *(looking toward bus):* Here it comes!

TYLER *(frantically):* I can't seem to find any quarters. *(Counting change)* I've got 5, 10, 15 cents. That's not enough, is it? *(Searches every pocket again)*

(As TYLER *is panicking,* DENNIS *kneels down, opens guitar case, and takes out loose change.)*

DENNIS *(handing change to* TYLER*):* Here. It's on me.

TYLER: Oh, no, I can't take money from you! That's ridiculous. Won't the driver take a check? It's guaranteed!

DENNIS: They won't even take gold bullion. Go figur'. Exact change only—no Canadian. If you don't take this money, you're going to miss your bus and it's a *long* walk to Wall Street.

TYLER *(still searching):* You know, the city really ought to consider taking MasterCard to cover local bus fares. You know, you could just zip your card through a little machine and, voilà! instant remuneration. Even grocery stores take plastic, for goodness' sake!

DENNIS *(continuing to hold out change):* I'm sure it's just a matter of time.

TYLER *(looking to see if anyone is watching, takes change):* Well, thank you. I'm afraid this is all the change you earned this morning.

DENNIS: Oh, there's more where that came from. *(Sighs, hesitates)* Ah! You know, you're right! It does feel good to help someone less fortunate than yourself.

Curtain

It's in There!

Theme: Blessed Are Those Who Have Not Seen

Scripture: John 20:19-31

Synopsis: So how do we know that God's love is there for us if we can't see it with our own two eyes? "Blessed are those who have not seen and have yet believed." We know by the witnesses to our belief—the effects of our belief. We see the result. How do we trust that what we believe is true? It only takes a small portion of willingness on our part for the Holy Spirit to teach us of His presence. With faith the size of a mustard seed, our lives, like the seed, will begin their transformation. And we will see the witness of God's presence in our lives as others respond to the Spirit shining from within us.

Cast:
> JIM*
> ANN*
> CUSTOMERS
> *Not gender specific

Props:
> Various size flowerpots filled with dirt
> Table
> Play money
> Sign, "FLOWERS FOR SALE"

Setting: A city sidewalk

(There is a table with a display of pots containing dirt. In front of the table is a sign that says "FLOWERS FOR SALE." JIM stands behind the table selling his wares. As the scene opens, a couple of people are at the stand. They give JIM some money and leave happily with a pot of dirt.)

JIM: Get your fresh flowers right here. Petunias, pansies, lobelia. You name it—we've got it!

(CUSTOMERS look and pass by without buying. ANN enters, slumped over, unhappy. Crosses in front of stand.)

JIM: Now, *you* look like someone who could use a little cheering up.

ANN *(looks to see if he's talking to someone else):* You talking to me?

JIM: Yes, you. The person with the little gray cloud above your head.

ANN *(looks up as if true):* There's no dark cloud following me. I'm just fine. *(Starts to leave)*

JIM *(calling after her):* Wait a minute! I've got just what you need.

ANN *(stopping again):* Look, buddy, flowers are OK, but they're just plants. They're not some miraculous cure for depression. That's false advertising. *(Crossing to display)* And speaking of false advertising, how do you

13

get away with calling these "flowers." *(Lifts pot of dirt and examines it)* It looks more like dirt in a pot to me.

JIM: Oh, they're flowers, all right.

ANN: Look. *(Holding pot up)* Do you honestly see any flowers in this pot?

JIM *(looks, sighs):* Ah, beautiful. Calendula. My favorite.

ANN *(looking at pot):* You're nuts.

JIM: What do you mean? These are calendula. Don't you believe me?

ANN: I think you may have spent a little too much time in the greenhouse. I know what flowers look like. They have stems and petals. They're colorful and showy. I've seen them with my own two eyes. *(Emphatically)* This is dirt.

JIM: Oh. I see. You insist on *seeing* the flowers before you'll believe they are there.

ANN: Well, of course I do. Doesn't everybody?

JIM: Actually, no. Some people believe me when I tell them these are flowers. They look forward to the emergence of the delicate sprout. They believe, when they see the first leaves, that a bloom will follow.

ANN: Well, even I can convince myself that a flower might come from a little sprout. But I don't even see a speck of green here. How do I know there's even a seed in here? You could well be selling plain old dirt.

JIM: Oh, there's a seed in there, all right.

ANN: But how do I know for *sure* there's a seed in there?

JIM: Because I just told you there was.

ANN: But why should I believe you? You're just a flower guy. Besides, you said you had what I needed. I don't need a pot of dirt—with or without any seeds in it.

JIM: You're right. You don't need the dirt *or* the seed. It's the *belief* in the seed that you need.

ANN: Pardon me?

JIM: You don't believe in anything you can't see and, considering how little we are actually able to see into this world, you don't believe in much.

ANN: So? There's nothing wrong with wanting to be certain about things. I just need proof, that's all.

JIM: But what can you actually be certain about? *(Looks into pot)* I am certain that right now, although I cannot see it happening, a seed is being transformed in this dirt. In a short time, I will see a little sprout emerge, and this sprout will be a witness to what I have been believing all along—the seed is there. And from the sprout will come leaves and buds. The tender plant will need tending and nurturing to grow. As it becomes strong, I know there will appear a bloom, a beautiful bloom, and this will be my reward for believing in the seed.

ANN (*staring into pot*): You see all that in this pot of dirt?

JIM: Sure. But you can't see it with your eyes. You've got to dig a little deeper. You have to look with your heart.

ANN (*continues staring into pot; pauses*): Hey, I think I see something. This is . . . this is . . . impatiens!

JIM: Could be.

ANN (*picking up another pot*): And this looks like . . . daisies!

JIM: Entirely possible.

ANN: This is amazing! I believe in something I can't even see. (*With sudden enthusiasm*) I'll take them. I'll take this one and this one and how about, this one. (*Snatches up the pots*)

JIM: My, you're a fast learner.

ANN (*pausing, deliberate consideration*): Yes, I believe I am.

Curtain

Make It Move

Theme: Faith As Small as a Mustard Seed

Scripture: Luke 17:5-10

Synopsis: According to this saying attributed to Jesus, our faith is a critically important element in our development. Our faith in everything—good and bad—must be examined carefully because our faith has the power to affect everything in our lives. And yet our free will enables us to choose what it is we put our faith in. By putting our faith in the power of God's will, we will surely move mountains. Actually watching them move before our eyes is not guaranteed nor critical to God's final outcome.

Cast:
ACTOR 1*
ACTOR 2*
JANITOR* (nonspeaking part)
*Not gender specific

Props:
2 folding chairs
Bible
Tape measure
Broom

Setting: There are two folding chairs placed at odd angles on the stage. The stage area doesn't represent any particular kind of room or place.

(ACTOR 1 *enters, in deep contemplation, reading his [her] Bible. Reaching center stage, he reads out loud.*)

ACTOR 1: "If you have faith as small as a mustard seed, you can say to this mulberry tree, 'Be uprooted and planted in the sea,' and it will obey you." (*Looks up; pauses*) " . . . and it will obey you." (*Pause*) Nah! It can't be true.

(ACTOR 1 *starts to exit, stops suddenly, and slowly turns around. Pauses to look around room for something to "move," finally deciding on one of the two chairs. He repositions the DS chair, studies it, crosses to the US chair, and sits facing the congregation and DS chair. Begins to stare at DS chair, intensely. ACTOR 2 enters as though passing through. Attention is caught by ACTOR 1 staring at chair. ACTOR 2 slowly backs up, moving to stand next to ACTOR 1, and studies same DS chair. Pauses. ACTOR 1 continues to concentrate.*)

ACTOR 2 (*stage whisper*): I don't get it. What's so fascinating?

ACTOR 1 (*still staring*): I'm making it move.

ACTOR 2: Really? How far has it come?

ACTOR 1 *(breaks concentration):* Oh, this is ridiculous! A person can't make a chair move just by willing it to.

ACTOR 2: You mean you thought you could move it through mental telepathy or something? Sheesh. What books have you been reading?

ACTOR 1: This one. *(Hands* ACTOR 2 *a Bible)* And I'm not trying to move it through mental telepathy—I'm trying to move it by *faith.*

ACTOR 2: What are you talking about?

ACTOR 1 *(standing, turns to find scripture passage):* Look, here . . . here in Luke 17. *(Reading with emphasis)* "If you have faith as small as a mustard seed, you can say to this mulberry tree, 'Be uprooted and planted in the sea,' and it will obey you." See, right there.

ACTOR 2: I don't see anything in here about a chair.

ACTOR 1 *(ignoring remark):* A mustard seed! A mustard seed! Do you know how small a mustard seed is? It's like one of the tiniest seeds on earth. Smaller than a sesame seed! It's minuscule. It's like a poppy seed. And it says here that's all the faith you need to make a mulberry tree jump out of the ground and land in the sea somewhere.

ACTOR 2 *(leafing through Bible):* I thought it said something about moving a mountain to a molehill.

ACTOR 1 *(not listening):* And I can't even move this chair an inch. Do you know what that means?

ACTOR 2: You should have started out with something smaller?

ACTOR 1: It means I have *no faith!* Zip! Zero! Nada! Not even this much. *(Pinches fingers together, indicating size of a mustard seed)*

ACTOR 2: Maybe something was lost in the translation. Maybe what Jesus really said was that if you have faith the size of a mountain you can move a mustard seed. That sounds more reasonable.

ACTOR 1: It's not just me, you know. I've never seen anyone actually move a mulberry tree. Have you?

ACTOR 2: I'm not even sure I've seen a mulberry tree.

ACTOR 1: So what is this scripture saying? Does it mean that it's impossible to have faith at all?

ACTOR 2: Well, what exactly is "faith"?

ACTOR 1: It's like, what you believe. If you believe this much in something *(pinching fingers together),* you can make it happen.

ACTOR 2: So, movable chairs aside, what *do* you believe in?

ACTOR 1: What do I believe in?

ACTOR 2: Yeah. What can you honestly say you believe in—without a shadow of a doubt?

ACTOR 1: OK. *(Pausing, then with certainty)* Without a shadow of a doubt, I can say that I believe the sun will rise every day.

ACTOR 2: And does it?

ACTOR 1: Of course it does! What sort of question is that?

ACTOR 2: Well, which came first—the sun rising or your belief in the sun rising? *(Pauses)* What else do you believe in without a shadow of a doubt?

ACTOR 1 *(pausing, again with certainty)*: All right. I can honestly say, without a shadow of a doubt, that I believe in gravity.

ACTOR 2: So which came first? Gravity—or your *belief* in gravity?

ACTOR 1: Is this a trick question like which came first—the chicken or the egg?

ACTOR 2: Answer me this. Do you believe in sickness? Do you believe in death?

ACTOR 1: Oh, come on. I don't know that I "believe" in sickness and death, but they happen whether I believe in them or not.

ACTOR 2: But, what if you didn't believe or "have faith" in them. Would death and sickness still happen?

ACTOR 1: So, you're saying that I don't really believe I can move this chair. Is that it?

ACTOR 2: That's right. You believe in a lot of things, but moving that chair is not one of them.

ACTOR 1: Well, you just watch this! *(Sits in chair and focuses all attention on moving chair. Pauses to concentrate.)*

(At the same time, ACTOR 2 crosses to DS chair, waiting with tape measure for chair to move. After appropriate pause, ACTOR 2 gets down on all fours and measures the distance chair has moved. ACTOR 1 looks hopeful. ACTOR 2 shakes his [her] head no.)

ACTOR 2: Sorry. It didn't move a millimeter.

ACTOR 1: Well, that's it. *(Dejected)* I must be completely faithless!

(ACTOR 2 consoles ACTOR 1 as they begin to exit down a center or side aisle.)

ACTOR 2: Maybe you should take a nap and try again later.

ACTOR 1: Yeah, you're right. You'd be surprised how exhausting it is to try to have that much faith in something.

(As ACTORS 1 and 2 turn their backs to exit, a JANITOR enters with broom and crosses stage unnoticed. Beginning to sweep, he [she] notices chair sitting out, crosses to chair, and carries it offstage.)

Curtain

Stranger in the Night

Theme: The Woman at the Well

Scripture: John 4:5-42

Synopsis: Once more we see Jesus addressing the marginalized person in the story of the woman at the well in Samaria. There are many aspects of this story that deserve focus. I have illustrated a few of the key elements in the story in hopes that you can use them as a springboard to discuss this story in further depth. Jesus was in Samaria—a place of impurity in the eyes of Jews. Jesus spoke with a Samaritan woman—two strikes against her—origin and gender. But He knew this person, regardless of her own perceived status or lack of status by society's measure, Jesus knew her. He met her on the fringe under her own circumstances—the water well at noon. All the "respectable" women retrieved water early, in the cool of morning. The woman considered herself a "marginal" person. She believed what others believed about her. She had no context of her own in which to see herself as someone of worth. But Jesus gave her a new context. Jesus gave her the opportunity for a life fresh from God.

Cast:

JESS: *a calm, caring man*
CHRIS: *Jess's friend (male or female)*
ROSE: *a woman, plainly dressed, carrying a sack lunch*

Props:

Bench
Grocery sack
Box of Pop-Tarts

Setting: A bus stop on a city street

(JESS *and* CHRIS *enter the street and move toward the bench to wait for a bus.* JESS *appears calm, but* CHRIS *is obviously anxious, looking all around for impending danger.)*

CHRIS: Why on earth did we have to come this way? Especially at night. This neighborhood gives me the creeps.

JESS: Oh, come on. It's not so bad.

CHRIS: Why'd I let you talk me into this. I don't want to ride the bus. We can just take a cab. That would be a lot safer and quicker. Come on, I'll pay for it!

JESS: Settle down, Chris. You're starting to hyperventilate. We're fine. Don't assume something terrible's going to happen. We'll just catch the next bus and be on our way. No big deal. We're just passing through.

CHRIS: Well, I'm sorry if I don't feel as comfortable on these streets as you do. I prefer well-lit streets with a couple of cops on horseback and a few more on foot. Look around. There's no one here. The streets are abandoned. It's as if everyone knows it's not safe to be out except us tourists. I'm getting a cab. *(Yells)* Taxi! (JESS *sits.)* Taxi! Oh, good. This one's stopping. *(Relieved)* We're out of here.

JESS: You go on. I'm going to take the bus.

CHRIS: What? *(To imaginary cab driver)* Wait just a second, would you? Don't leave, OK? I'm going with you! *(To JESS)* Are you crazy? I've got a taxi right here. Let's go. We'll be out of this neighborhood in no time.

JESS: You go ahead. I'm fine. I'll see you later.

CHRIS *(to cab driver):* Just one more second, OK? Don't leave! *(To JESS)* I'm not kidding, Jess. I'm leaving. I don't want to leave you alone, but I'm outta here.

JESS: Go on. No problem. Don't feel bad about leaving. I understand, really.

CHRIS *(reluctant):* OK. I'm leaving. I'm getting into this cab, and I'm going home.

JESS: See you later.

CHRIS: The bus may not be here for another half an hour!

JESS: I'll be fine.

CHRIS: OK. It's your funeral. I've done what I can. Don't say I didn't warn you!

(CHRIS *exits as if to cab.* ROSE *enters carrying a grocery sack. Also waiting for bus. Sees* JESS *and is uncomfortable with his presence. She sits at farthest edge of bench, ignoring* JESS.)

JESS *(talking to but not looking at* ROSE): It's a nice night.

ROSE *(startled, clutches her sack tightly):* You talking to me?

JESS: Of course I'm talking to you. Who else would I be talking to?

ROSE *(looking around):* Maybe you're talking to yourself. A lot of people around here do, you know.

JESS: Really? That's interesting. No. I was talking to you. *(Pause)* Nice night, huh?

ROSE *(uncomfortable):* I suppose. *(Looking away)*

JESS *(not looking at* ROSE): Boy, I sure am hungry.

(ROSE *squirms in her seat, uncomfortable with this stranger speaking to her.)*

JESS: I don't suppose I could buy something from you, could I? It looks like you've been shopping for groceries.

ROSE *(looking in sack):* How do you know?

JESS: Just a guess. Do you have an extra banana—even a piece of bread would do. I've got money. *(Takes out a dollar, handing it to her)*

ROSE *(not wanting to talk, looks through sack halfheartedly):* Nope. I ain't got nothing extra.

Jess: Nothing? Are you sure?

Rose *(giving in):* Oh, OK . . . what about a Pop-Tart? Is that OK? I'll give you one Pop-Tart, but that's all.

Jess: That would be fine, thank you.

(Rose *opens box of Pop-Tarts and hands a package to* Jess.)

Rose: There. *(Sarcastically)* You don't mind frosting, do you?

Jess: Frosting's fine. Thank you. You're very generous. *(Pause)* Why do you do your shopping so late?

Rose *(uncomfortable):* I just do. There's less people around, that's all. Shorter lines. What's it to you?

Jess: Your husband doesn't mind you going out by yourself this late?

Rose *(pausing):* He don't care.

Jess: You don't have a husband, do you?

Rose: Hey, it's none of your business if I have a husband or don't have a husband. You're awful nosy for someone I've never even seen around before. You should learn when to keep your mouth shut. You don't belong around here, that's for sure.

Jess: I'm just passing through.

Rose: Well, why do you ask so many questions about people?

Jess: I'm just interested, that's all. I've never met a person I didn't like.

Rose: Well, that proves you ain't from around here!

Jess: You're a nice person, Rose.

Rose: How'd you know my name? I didn't tell you my name!

Jess: I think you must have.

Rose: Oh, no I didn't! I don't tell no stranger who I am.

Jess: Well, no harm done. I just said you're a nice person. You're kind. You gave a stranger a Pop-Tart. You didn't have to do that.

Rose: You practically begged me. Besides, I was trying to make you shut up.

Jess: I think you were being thoughtful. That's the kind of person you are.

Rose: You don't know me. I ain't so nice as you say.

Jess: I know you don't think you are. You lied to me about your husband. You don't live with your husband, do you?

Rose *(surprised and uncomfortable):* So what if I don't. You wouldn't want to live with my husband either. *(Stands quickly, looking for bus)* When's that bus coming! It gets later every night, I swear!

Jess: You deserve to be treated well, Rose. You deserve love in your life. You deserve respect, you know. Don't ever believe otherwise. When you look at yourself in the mirror each morning, you do what I do and tell yourself that you are a person who deserves to give and receive real love, OK? 'Cause I know you, Rose. Maybe I know you better than you know yourself.

ROSE (*staring in disbelief, speaks softly in stage whisper*): I've never even seen you before.

JESS (*stands, looking for bus*): Hey, I think I see the bus coming. It was nice talking to you, Rose, and thanks again for the Pop-Tart. I'll always remember your kindness.

(JESS *exits as if toward bus.* ROSE *stares after him in disbelief, not moving from bench. When* JESS *has exited,* ROSE *speaks line.*)

ROSE: You're welcome.

Curtain

Trust Me

Theme: The Temptation of Christ

Scripture: Matthew 4:1-11

Synopsis: In the New Testament Greek, the translation for "devil" is "the slanderer." I think this image of that mystery we call the devil is extremely helpful for our understanding of the way this negative energy works around us. It is the Untruth—just as God is the Truth. It speaks lies to us on a daily basis and will take every opportunity to slip an untruth in our ear. The Truth makes us whole and strong—effective instruments for Christ. The Untruth breaks us—often with pretty lies—but always, in the end, it seeks to separate us from God's love. We must focus on the voice of Truth as Jesus did in Matthew's story of Christ's temptation. The slanderer whispered pretty lies to Jesus, but He held to the Truth. This must be a model for our own survival if we are to be nourished by the true hand of God. *One last note:* The scripture says that the Spirit led Jesus into the wilderness; it never said the Spirit left Him alone there.

Cast:
    SHERRY: *Tracy's slightly intimidating date for the evening*
    TRACY: *not completely lacking in confidence, but this date has him flustered*
    MAN: *supercasual person, the embodiment of Tracy's tempter*

Props:
    2 chairs
    Table

SFX: Doorbell

Setting: A home or apartment

(There are two chairs and a table [dining room setting would work well]. As the scene begins, SHERRY *is preparing to go out. We hear a doorbell ring.* SHERRY *answers the door.)*

SHERRY: Hi, Tracy. You're right on time. I'm almost ready.

*(*TRACY *follows* SHERRY.*)*

SHERRY: I just need to feed the cat before we go. *(As she exits)* I hope you're not allergic.

TRACY *(calling to* SHERRY; *nervous but wanting to impress):* Oh no, I love cats. Just love them. *(Looking around apartment)* Can't get enough of them, actually.

SHERRY *(returning):* Oh, do you have a cat?

TRACY: Well, no, not at the moment. But I love them. I just . . . really . . . love them.

SHERRY: I can't stand them, myself. I'm just cat-sitting for my sister. I'm more of a dog person, really.

TRACY (*changing tune suddenly*): Oh, well, dogs! Who doesn't like dogs? Dogs are great. Now if I *did* have a pet, it would be a dog. That's for sure. I love dogs, all right.

SHERRY: What kind?

TRACY (*surprised*): Pardon?

SHERRY: What kind . . . what breed would you choose if you could have any kind of dog? A big breed—like a Great Dane, or a Borzoi?

TRACY: Oh, sure, big dogs are great. The more foreign the better. (*Regretting conversation*) You can really . . . wrestle with a big dog and pal around, you know, Lassie, ol' Yeller, Rin Tin Tin . . .

SHERRY (*disappointed*): So . . . you like big, slobbery dogs, huh?

TRACY (*sensing disapproval*): Well, not *really*. Did I give you that impression? Big dogs are OK, but give me a lapdog any day. Small dogs are great companions, and you can take them anywhere—airplanes, grocery carts. When they ride in cars they stick their cute little faces out the driver's window, ears flapping in the wind . . .

SHERRY (*not revealing own opinion*): Interesting. (*Changing subject*) Well, the movie starts in half an hour. We'd better get going. I'll grab my coat. There's some beer and wine in the fridge if you want a drink before we go. (*Exits*)

(TRACY *smiles until she's out of sight. Frustrated, he whops himself on the forehead with the palm of his hand several times—à la Charlie Brown. During monologue, MAN slinks in, unnoticed. He is dressed in a slick suit—cool and self-assured.*)

TRACY (*to himself*): Dumb, dumb, dumb. What am I talking about? Cats . . . dogs. I sound ridiculous! Who do I think I am—a veterinarian, for heaven's sake? Oh, she must think I'm a dunce. (*Gets idea*) Maybe I should just sneak out while she's out of the room. Yeah, that's what I'll do. It'll be easier for everyone in the long run. (*Pause*) No, I can't do that. I'll never be able to face another woman again in my whole life if I leave now. I just need to pull myself together. I can handle this. Deep cleansing breaths, deep cleansing breaths . . .

MAN (*calmly*): Why don't you have that drink she offered you?

TRACY (*notices MAN for the first time*): You! What are you doing here? I don't need your help on this.

MAN (*amused*): Oh, I think you do. (*Quoting*) "There's nothing like a good lapdog?" Oh, really, Tracy. You've floundered before, but this is bad. You're sinking fast, buddy. (*Whispering in his ear*) She intimidates the pants off you, doesn't she?

TRACY (*pumping himself up*): No. Why would she intimidate me? I'm cool. I'm a with-it kind of guy. I've got nothing to be ashamed of. Women like me.

MAN: Sure they do. They love you—when you're relaxed and calm. You just need to slow down a bit. Why don't you reconsider that drink she offered? That would help you feel more comfortable.

TRACY: Stop it. I don't want to hear this. You know I can't . . .

MAN (interrupting): Just one little drink won't hurt. Come on. It'll make you feel like a man. It'll give you that boost of confidence you need. Just a little . . . bitty . . . drink. Trust me.

(MAN trying to hypnotize TRACY and succeeding, until Tracy breaks away. MAN's movements are flowing and snakelike.)

TRACY: No! You know what alcohol does to me! Get out of here. You don't really care about me. I'll do this alone.

MAN: Oh, come now. You can't do this alone—you never could—and I *do* care about you. You don't seem to understand that. I'm the only one who really wants you to be happy. I'm the only one you can trust. You can't deny how good a beer would make you feel right now, can you?

TRACY (fighting temptation): There's more to life than getting high. There are other things that can make you feel good.

MAN (amused): Like what?

TRACY (struggling): Like . . . like . . . like relationships! Good friendships! Nature—sunshine, flowers.

MAN: Oh, please. (Sarcastically) Joy of joys, it's a sunny day. Look at the flowers blooming as the cheerful little bunnies hop to and fro . . . Gag me.

TRACY: OK, so that sounds a little like a Hallmark card, but it's true. Love is real, and I want to be guided by the Truth now—not by you! So go—beat it. Leave me alone.

MAN (unshaken): Oh dear, ladies and gentlemen, I do believe he's serious this time. Well, we'll see. I'll leave you now before you throw a bucket of water on me. But, for your information, I won't melt away like M & M's in the sweaty hand of a child. (Slowly) I'll be back.

(MAN exits as SHERRY enters. They pass each other, but she cannot see him.)

SHERRY: Sorry that took so long. The cat knocked over her milk dish, and I had to clean it up. She's not so bad—kind of friendly, really. Did you help yourself to a drink?

TRACY: No. (Gaining courage) Actually, Sherry, I don't drink alcohol—ever. I hope you're OK with that.

SHERRY (surprised by his honesty; begins to exit): Sure. That's fine. I don't drink often myself. (Slight pause) What about espresso?

TRACY (starts to answer, realizes he may end up backtracking as before; picks a different tact): Espresso? Why don't you tell me how you feel about it first.

Curtain

Make Amends

Theme: Resolving Anger

Scripture: Matthew 5:21-37

Synopsis: Certainly, this is a tough saying of Jesus. "Go and be reconciled to your brother; then come and offer your gift." In the preceding passage, Jesus equates anger with murder. We can see that anger in varying degrees is murder that is not acted upon, but it still swells in the heart, condemning those we hold anger toward. When we harbor anger we are choosing to look at someone in a way different from the way God looks at them. Usually anger is accompanied by self-righteousness. So, actually, we feel proud of the fact that we are unloving. This is such an important passage for preparation to worship. Wouldn't it be incredible if we all obeyed the words of Jesus and sought to purify our relationships in a way that would please God, and then, with clean slates, enter before God in true humility and purity? How might this change the face of Christ's Church?

Cast:
> ACTOR 1*
> ACTOR 2*
> *Not gender specific

Props:
> Small table
> 2 chairs
> Wastebasket
> Crumpled letter
> Box of Kleenex

Setting: A family home

(Two adult family members are preparing to go to church. ACTOR 1 and ACTOR 2 are not given gender, so as not to appear to be stereotyping anyone. There is a small table and two chairs. Next to the table is a small wastebasket with a crumpled up letter in it. At rise, ACTOR 1 is sitting in a chair ready to go to church. He [she] is obviously impatient and has been waiting several minutes.)

ACTOR 1 *(shouting to someone offstage):* Are you ready yet? I'm falling asleep in here!

ACTOR 2 *(offstage):* Coming. Just one more thing.

ACTOR 1 *(exasperated):* We're going to be late again!

ACTOR 2 *(enters with coat on):* We haven't been late to church in 20 years, and we won't be late today. You don't even have your coat on yet.

ACTOR 1: I was waiting for you!

ACTOR 2: Well, I'm here, and we still have half an hour before the service starts. Now get your coat on.

ACTOR 1: Half an hour! If we're not there 20 minutes early, Joe and Mary Smellner take our pew and we end up in the back row where you can't see the choir. There's no respect for a person's pew anymore. There used to be respect for a person's pew, but no more!

ACTOR 2: It's not your own personal pew. If you want your own pew, you ought to keep one at home and take it in with you on Sunday morning.

ACTOR 1 (preparing to leave): Very funny. Like a pew would actually fit in the trunk of the Buick. Let's go.

ACTOR 2: Just a second. I need some Kleenex. (ACTOR 2 crosses behind chair, notices the crumpled up letter in the wastebasket. Pauses to look at it.)

ACTOR 1: They've got Kleenex at the church, you know. What do you think all those offerings go for? They buy Kleenex. Now, let's get going.

(ACTOR 1 begins to exit as ACTOR 2 picks up crumpled letter and unfolds it.)

ACTOR 2: What's this? (Reading letter)

ACTOR 1 (not paying attention): What's what? Probably junk mail. I'm walking out the door. I'm opening the door. All the heat is escaping . . .

ACTOR 2: This is a letter about your family's reunion this spring. What's it doing in the wastebasket?

ACTOR 1 (caught): Uh, I don't know. How could it have gotten there? (Lightly) Oh well, let's go.

ACTOR 2 (reading): Oh my. Look at all the people who are planning to attend—Cousin Karen from Redding, Great-Aunt Rose all the way from Lakeland, Florida, your brother Carl from Atlanta . . . (Pause) You threw this letter away, didn't you?

ACTOR 1: What? Me? I've never seen that letter before in my life.

ACTOR 2: You threw away your own family—right into that wastebasket there.

ACTOR 1: Oh, you mean, did I throw away that letter? Well, I don't know, maybe. Maybe I thought it was something about getting our family tree drawn up. You know it could have been some ripoff "family heritage" scheme of some kind. You can't be too careful these days.

ACTOR 2: You're pathetic. Throwing away your own flesh and blood like that. And I know why too. You read that your brother, Carl, was going to be there, and you don't want to see him, right? You're still holding that ancient grudge against your own brother! What was it? Some argument about who caught the biggest fish on that Westport trip? Wasn't that it?

ACTOR 1 (to self): I can see Joe Smellner easing into my pew at this very moment. He's picking up my hymnal and using my pencil to sign himself in.

ACTOR 2: When are you going to get over this infantile feud? What will it take? You've given up your brother because of some silly flounder.

ACTOR 1: That was no "silly flounder"! That was a 60-pound halibut, and I reeled him in! Carl says we only caught him because of his expert netting technique. Well, I'll tell you—a netter isn't worth anything if the fish isn't reeled in! Come on. Can't we talk about this later, after a nice quiet brunch at the Country Buffet?

ACTOR 2: Didn't you hear what Pastor Roberts said last week?

ACTOR 1: You mean about the bowling league?

ACTOR 2: No.

ACTOR 1: Oh, you mean about the desperate need for Sunday School teachers?

ACTOR 2: No! During the sermon—what he said during the sermon!

ACTOR 1: No, I guess I was resting my eyes at that point and didn't hear anything.

ACTOR 2: Well, he said that you're not supposed to go to church to worship God until you've made amends with all those people you hold hard feelings against.

ACTOR 1: You mean like people you've argued with or people you don't like? Ha, the church would be empty if everyone had to make apologies before they could come to a service. *(Amused)*

ACTOR 2: Well, that's what Pastor told us. Jesus said it in the Bible. *(Paraphrasing)* Um, "make up with your brothers and sisters before you bring your offering to the altar"—otherwise, your worship doesn't do any good.

ACTOR 1: Oh, come on. You mean God would rather have me home talking to my brother on the phone than sitting in my pew like a good Christian? I've never heard any preacher say that!

ACTOR 2: That's exactly what Pastor said. You better get on that phone and make up with your brother before we step one foot into God's house.

ACTOR 1 *(pausing):* I'll write him a letter this afternoon. *(Starts to exit)*

(As ACTOR 1 exits, ACTOR 2 sits down at table. ACTOR 1 reenters.)

ACTOR 1: What are you doing now?

ACTOR 2 *(calmly):* I can't go.

ACTOR 1: What are you talking about? This isn't even your problem. So maybe my being in church today won't count, but you haven't missed a Sunday service in 30 years!

ACTOR 2: Well, maybe I should have. Maybe I should have cleaned my slate a few times before I pretended that my heart was pure and ready to listen to God's Word.

ACTOR 1 *(exasperated):* You really think God would rather I take time to talk to my brother than keep my perfect attendance record?

ACTOR 2: If it meant that you would be willing to show love toward someone God loves, I know He would.

ACTOR 1: But, this is going to be *really* hard to do. I haven't talked to Carl for . . .

ACTOR 2: It doesn't matter. You can talk to him right now.

ACTOR 1 *(pausing):* Do I have to? I don't know what to say. It's embarrassing to apologize to someone.

ACTOR 2: I know, but it's good for us. Pastor said it "frees us to worship."

ACTOR 1: Oh, all right. If it means I get my pew back, I'll do it.

ACTOR 2: I think you'll get a lot more than a pew out of this.

(Exit)

Curtain

The Son Shines Bright

Theme: I Have Come That They May Have Life

Scripture: John 10:1-10

Synopsis: Jesus came that we might have life and have it abundantly. Maybe we've never shut ourselves up in a basement or glued ourselves to the television for three days, but how *do* we choose to turn away from the abundant life that is offered by Christ? How do we resist all that is held out to us? Depression is rampant in our society. Jesus says we can turn our life of burdens into a burden of light.

Cast:
> JIM*: *has shut himself up in the basement for three days*
> ANDI*: *a friend or family member who enters into the dark mess*
> *Not gender specific

Props:
> Comfortable lounge chair
> Coffee table or end table
> Remote control (for TV)
> Snack bags, some open
> Magazines and papers
> 2 pair of sunglasses

Setting: The basement of a house

(There is a comfortable chair and a table with a remote control and a mess of eaten snacks on it and the floor. The basement is supposed to be dark except for the glow of the TV. If you have no lighting effects, the actors will need to portray this effect by their actions. At rise, JIM is slouching in the lounge chair pointing the remote toward the congregation and imaginary TV.)

ANDI *(entering, steps over unidentifiable debris):* Jim? Jim, are you down here? *(Hears grunt)* Is that you, Jim? I can't see anything except the TV. Are you down here? *(Another grunt)* This is disgusting. *(Picks up trash, examines it closely, reacting in disgust)* Where are you, Jim? Are you still breathing, buddy? *(Crosses to chair)* It's so dark down here. Where's the light switch?

JIM *(in monotone):* I don't want any light on!

ANDI: Hallelujah. You're alive. I think. At least I hear your voice.

(ANDI stands directly in front of JIM with back to the congregation—between JIM and TV.)

JIM: Hey! Do you mind? I'm watching something very important here!

ANDI *(turns to look at TV):* The Home Shopping Network?

JIM: Get out of the way. There are only 102 authentically, simulated zirconium anniversary rings left, and I'm seriously thinking of ordering one!

ANDI: You're thinking about buying a zirconium anniversary ring?

JIM: Maybe. It's a great bargain, and I've never had one before. *(Entranced)* Look how it sparkles. I've never seen anything sparkle like that.

ANDI: Jim—earth calling Jim—you're not even married! You don't need an anniversary ring if you don't have any anniversaries! What are you doing down here? This is some serious hibernating! You've been shut up in this dark basement for three days now. Don't you think it's about time you came out.

JIM: What for?

ANDI: What for? To see the daylight, maybe? To get some fresh air. To talk to another human being instead of staring at that inane television all the time.

JIM: Hey, now you're getting personal. This television is my friend. I can depend on this television. If this TV tells me that *The Andy Griffith Show* is coming up next, well, you can bet your bottom dollar that you're going to see Barney and Goober after the next commercial. You can depend on television.

ANDI: What is it, Jim? Are you depressed? Should I call for some professional help?

JIM: What depressed? I *like* it down here. It's quiet. No one bugs me—well, not till you came, anyway. Can't a person in this democratic society shut themselves away from everything for a few days and not end up on *The Rickie Lake Show*? I'm happy enough. Just leave me alone. Oh no, only 97 rings left. They're selling like hotcakes!

ANDI: So, this is how you're going to live the rest of your life—sitting in the darkness letting an inanimate technical device program your thoughts?

JIM: What's it to you? I'm not bothering anyone. There are lots of people who shut themselves up against the world. Go bother them. Besides, it's cozy down here.

ANDI *(looking around)*: It's disgusting down here. *(Wipes off chair and sits)* You might consider taking the garbage out once in awhile. I know moles that live better than this.

JIM: Oh, you get used to it. Look at that—only 75 rings left! What should I do? What should I do?

ANDI: You should wake up and smell the coffee! You need some sunlight, my friend. Come on, let's go for a walk around the block. It'll give you a new outlook on things. *(Trying to entice)* There are trees out there, and flowers. Real life can be pretty exciting if you give it a chance.

JIM *(defensively): This* is real life. I'm alive, aren't I?

ANDI: Well, I hear you talking, so I know your heart must be beating, but I'm not sure this qualifies as "real life."

JIM: Oh, come on. Do you realize that the majority of animal life on earth functions during the hours of darkness?

ANDI: Well, that's fine for bats and raccoons. But do you know what happens to those fish that live their entire lives in caves? They lose their sight completely! They become totally blind because they have no use for their vision in the dark.

JIM: You've been reading too many *National Geographic* magazines.

ANDI: My point is: human life should not be lived in darkness. We are not nocturnal! Our lives should be lived in the light. You don't experience life by being bombarded with intangible television images all the time—but by interacting with everything around you. By being an active part of creation. All you're creating down here is a mess.

JIM: Doesn't that count for anything?

ANDI: I think there's more out there for you, Jim, but you've got to start by changing your point of view. There's more waiting for you than a simulated zirconium anniversary ring.

JIM *(watching TV):* I sure hope you're right about that. They just sold the last one. *(Mocking anguish)* I missed out again!

ANDI: Don't worry about it. Let's get out of here and find something that's really worth celebrating. What do you say?

JIM: But I'm so comfortable down here. I don't know what to do up there.

ANDI: If you are just willing to take the first step, I promise, the rest will come to you.

JIM *(clicks "off" TV):* All right. I'll go, if you go with me. *(Pulls out sunglasses and puts them on)* Is it OK to wear these?

ANDI: Sure. The sun shines bright up there. *(Pulls out sunglasses, puts them on)* You just take it at your own pace, and I'll be with you every step of the way.

JIM *(stands and gropes around to find the door):* Are we there yet?

(ANDI leads him out.)

Curtain

Opportunities 'R' Us

Theme: The Cost of Being a Disciple

Scripture: Luke 14:25-33

Synopsis: From how comfortable we look on Sunday morning, you might not be able to tell that Jesus calls us to take the hard road. Jesus' words in this passage from Luke are not particularly kind and certainly not meant to coddle. They are challenging and powerful. They speak of risk taking and discomfort, of giving away all we have and of being willing to change what we think our life is about. How can we sit passively in the pew when we read these words and know that Jesus is speaking directly to us?

Cast:
> DALE*
> DIANE*
> *Not gender specific

Props:
> Desk or table
> 2 chairs
> Office paraphernalia, such as papers, telephone, files
> Manila envelope for résumé
> Sign: "Ministry Opportunities—God Needs YOU!"

Setting: A business office

(A desk or table and two chairs, a prominently displayed sign, "Ministry Opportunities—God Needs YOU!" There are papers, a telephone, and various office paraphernalia on the desk. DIANE enters carrying files. She settles herself at the desk as DALE pokes his head in the "office." He is carrying a manila envelope with his "résumé" in it.)

DALE: Excuse me. Is this the Ministry Opportunities office?

DIANE: Yes. You've come to the right place. Please, come in.

DALE *(enters nervously):* Um, I'm Dale. Dale Fenton.

DIANE *(stands to shake hands):* Hi, Dale. My name is Diane. It's nice to meet you, Dale. Come in and make yourself comfortable.

DALE: Oh, thanks. I hope I'm doing the right thing by coming into your office. To be quite honest with you, I'm not sure I'm ready for this.

DIANE: Well, that's fine. We can just talk a bit and explore some of your options. You don't have to commit to any ministry until you're ready. It's up to you.

DALE: OK. I'm only a layperson, you know.

DIANE: Don't say *"only* a layperson," Dale. Ministry is done by all God's people—most of whom are laypeople like you and me. Now, let me explain what we do here at Ministry Opportunities. After making a decision to follow Christ, a person will need and desire opportunities to serve God. That's where we come in. We help people discover their gifts and define their passions. The ministry you feel most passionate about might surprise you. For example, someone who works as an elementary schoolteacher during the week will not necessarily have a passion for teaching Sunday School. Perhaps God will lead that person to a visitation ministry or to be involved in the music program. Does that make sense to you, Dale?

DALE: I think so.

DIANE: We help people explore the possibilities and enable them to serve as they feel called. Now let's get back to you. You're feeling ready to serve?

DALE: Well, I think so. I've been working on the greatest commandment for quite a while—you know, loving God above all else—and I've been trying to love my neighbor as myself.

DIANE: That's great. Love is the place to start.

DALE: But recently I've felt like I want to do more. I want to get actively involved.

DIANE: Good. Do you have a particular ministry in mind?

DALE: Not really. *(Indicating envelope)* I brought my résumé.

DIANE: That's not necessary. We don't need to know your past experience to find a place for you. Let's just talk about what you like to do. Let's see. Have you thought about participating in the choir or the praise band?

(DIANE *works from a list, checking off unacceptable ministries.*)

DALE: I'm assuming that involves getting up in front of people.

DIANE: Yes, there is that requirement.

DALE: No, no. I don't want to do anything in front of people.

DIANE: Okay. So, no choir, no praise band, no drama ministry . . . (DALE *responds)* no scripture reading or children's message. No problem. There are a lot of other possibilities. What about ushering? Being an usher is a very important way to serve. The ushers assist in many ways; for example, they take the offering and make visitors feel at ease.

DALE: So, I'd have to talk to people, right?

DIANE: Yes, I imagine some conversation would be appropriate.

DALE: I'm afraid that's a little outside my comfort zone at this time.

DIANE: That's fine, Dale, and yet, sometimes serving God means that we stretch our comfort zone to discover new, exciting ways of participating. God will enable us to do great things like feeding people at the homeless shelter, *(insert ministries sponsored by your church)*, caring for infants and children, transporting an elderly person to a doctor's appointment, raising funds for new staff positions . . .

DALE: Couldn't I start off with something small and work my way up?

DIANE: Sure you can. I'll just refer to the opportunities list. Let's see here. You want to start small . . . *(Checking list)* I wouldn't say that any of these jobs are exactly "small." They're certainly not insignificant. What about transporting youth to various functions? That requires some time and a car.

DALE: No driver's license.

DIANE: OK. *(Pause)* What about helping wash dishes after a church dinner? That's not too risky, and it doesn't require a driver's license.

DALE: My hands chafe easily.

DIANE *(trying to remain cool)*: All right, Dale. There must be something here you can do . . . *(Checks list again)*

DALE: Make it something easy.

DIANE: Something easy?

DALE: Yeah, something easy that doesn't require a big time commitment or a lot of experience—no soapsuds, no driver's license, no homeless shelters, no children, and no standing up in front of people.

DIANE *(pausing)*: What about folding bulletins? You could do it in a quiet room all by yourself.

DALE: Can I do it once a month and get it done in less than an hour?

DIANE *(slowly)*: Dale, where did you ever get the idea that following Christ was going to be "easy"?

DALE: Well, I heard that everything gets better when you follow Jesus.

DIANE: Oh, life does get better, but it doesn't necessarily get easier. *(Stands, crosses slowly to behind DALE, making her point)* God wants something from you, Dale. God wants you to change the way you think, feel, and act toward people. *(Intensity builds)* And when you do change the way you think, feel, and act, you will also find the passion to serve others as Christ served. You might not be called to do something easy. You might have to get your hands dirty and give up some of your free time. You might even have to push the boundaries of your comfort zone to discover your true calling!

DALE *(applauding, speaks sincerely)*: That was a very inspiring speech.

DIANE *(composing herself)*: Well, I didn't mean to preach to you . . .

DALE: No, it's OK. You made me stop and think. Now it's clear to me what I should do.

DIANE: Really? That's marvelous. My little speech has never been the catalyst to such rapid change before. So, what job do you want? *(Prepares to write)*

DALE *(very excited)*: Yours! I want *your* job. It's perfect for me.

DIANE *(stunned)*: But, but, now, Dale . . .

DALE: Oh, I know it may seem like a bit of a stretch for me right now, having to talk to people and all, but you were right—we aren't called to do the easy thing, are we?

DIANE *(in disbelief):* But this is *my* job . . .

DALE *(not listening):* I feel great. I've finally found my calling, thanks to you! You can teach me everything you know. This is so exciting! And who knows, you might find a new way to serve. Maybe setting tables for potlucks or director of the Christmas pageant. Don't worry, I'll help you find something you feel passionate about. See you here first thing Monday morning to start my training! *(Exits)*

DIANE *(in a daze, spoken to herself as she exits):* Maybe I shouldn't be so emphatic about stretching the comfort zone. *(Fading)* After all, boundaries aren't so bad. We all need boundaries, right?

Curtain

This Is Your Life!

Theme: God of the Living

Scripture: Luke 20:27-38

Synopsis: In the passage from Luke, Jesus tells us that God is not the God of the dead, but the God of the living. Jesus refers to those great followers who have gone before Him—Abraham, Isaac, and Jacob, who dwell with God—alive! I think this statement sums up much of the message of Christ. God is the God of the *living*. God creates life, sustains life, and endorses life. We are brought into fullness of life through Christ, and it is God's will that we experience life fully. If it doesn't happen for us here on earth through the experience of Jesus Christ, then it will surely happen when we see God face-to-face. And yet, day to day, we take living for granted. In our crowded lives we do not seek vitality through the very energy of life, which is God. Yahweh is the God of the living. Yahweh is *our* God.

Cast:
> ERNIE
> EDNA

Props:
> Comfortable lounge chair
> Straight chair
> Coffee table
> Remote control
> Water glass

SFX: Phone ringing

Setting: A family home or apartment

(There is a comfortable chair [a reclining lounge chair if possible], a straight chair and a coffee table in between. The furniture is facing an imaginary TV and the audience. ERNIE enters and settles in the recliner. He is carrying a remote control. These two characters are elderly [they can be portrayed by younger actors playing older]. ERNIE takes a remote control out of his pocket and flips on the imaginary TV in front of him. He stares at it. EDNA passes across the stage. ERNIE stops her halfway but does not look up from the TV.)

ERNIE: We got any lemonade?

EDNA *(stopping):* In the fridge. *(Starts off)*

ERNIE: Well, as long as you're up . . .

EDNA *(stopping again, not pleased):* Oh, sure, your highness. I don't have anything else to do.

(EDNA exits. ERNIE stares at TV, holds hand out as if ready to grasp the glass of lemonade at any moment. EDNA reenters with glass. Seeing ERNIE's ready hand, deliberately puts lemonade on table. Reconsidering, she scoots it beyond his reach.)

EDNA: I thought you could use a little exercise.

ERNIE *(reaching for drink):* What exercise? Who needs exercise at my age. I'm 112 years old!

EDNA: You are not.

ERNIE: Well, I feel like 112.

EDNA: That's because you don't get any exercise. You sit in that chair like a vegetable. Half the time, I don't even know if you're dead or alive. Twice a day I check to see if you're still breathing.

ERNIE: Ah, I might as well be dead. My life's over anyway. If it weren't for *Jeopardy,* I'd have nothing to live for.

EDNA *(sits in straight chair, not really offended):* Well, thank you very much.

ERNIE: Ah, you've had me around for 50 years. That's enough for any sane person to take.

EDNA: It's been 75 years, you old coot, and for your information I'd just as soon keep you around a little longer, even though you are the crankiest thing on two legs. *(Studies him)* Well, maybe you're the crankiest thing on two cheeks.

ERNIE *(referring to show):* I can't hear the answers here, if you don't mind.

EDNA: Why do you waste your time on that *Jeopardy* show? You never know the answers.

ERNIE: The questions. You mean I never know the questions.

EDNA: Well, of course you don't know the questions. What are you, a mind-reader or something? You're getting delirious, old man. Why don't you get up out of that chair and *do* something. Take a walk. Paint the house. Climb a tree. Anything!

ERNIE: I'm too weak.

EDNA: You're not weak. You're just starting to atrophy. *(Trying another approach)* Well, if all you're going to do is sit around and watch game shows for the rest of your days, you might as well go now. Life is for the living, and you're taking up valuable space.

ERNIE: Well, if I thought they had high-quality television up in heaven, I just might consider going. But somehow I get the impression there's nothing much to do up there.

EDNA: So, you'll feel right at home.

ERNIE *(ignoring her):* Just a bunch of singing and floating around.

EDNA: That's because God has a thing about *living.* They're active up in heaven. They're *vital!* They're whooping it up!

ERNIE: Well, I don't have the energy to die.

EDNA: Oh, you've got the energy to die, all right. You're looking more and more like a wilted houseplant every day. What you don't have is the energy to *live!*

ERNIE: I've lived! You can't say I haven't lived! I've been living for 120 years.

EDNA: Give or take a few.

ERNIE: I've seen the invention of the motor car, the radio, the television, and the home satellite dish! I've been through two World Wars and countless international confrontations. I've outlived scores of presidents and matinee idols! I've paid off two mortgages and outlived my doctors. I have children and grandchildren, great-grandchildren, and even a few great-great-grandchildren! I think that's plenty of living for any one person, thank you very much!

EDNA: Well, I hate to tell you this, but you're not through yet. You may be acting like your life is over, but you've still got eternity to live through.

ERNIE: I'm too tired to live for eternity! I just want to watch a little *Jeopardy*, drink my lemonade, and relax. Am I asking too much?

(Phone rings. ERNIE *ignores it.* EDNA *answers.)*

EDNA: Hello. Yes, this is the Reardon residence. *(Listening)* You want to know if Ernie Reardon lives here? Just a minute, please. *(Studies* ERNIE, *who sits, staring at TV. Picks up his limp wrist and takes his pulse, then returns to phone.)* I can't tell. Maybe if you try back tomorrow I'll have a little better idea. Thanks for calling.

*(*EDNA *exits, leaving* ERNIE *sitting in chair staring at TV.)*

Curtain

Legally Ours

Theme: Blessings in Christ

Scripture: Ephesians 1:3-14

Synopsis: In the scripture from Ephesians, Paul says that it is God's pleasure and will that we are adopted as His children. God lavishes on us the riches of His grace freely and without limitation with all wisdom and understanding. God sees our beauty and our purity, and loves us as His children, and so we are. In "Legally Ours," the idea of what it means to become an adopted child is presented. Even in their humanness, the Clarks are inspired to share all they have with Jeff. There is nothing they will withhold from him, for he will be their son. It is their great joy to lavish Jeff with the graces that come from family membership. They see Jeff's goodness, and because this is what they see, it will be the light that leads him into adulthood; just as the perfect vision that God has of us lights our way to wholeness. A question that might be asked following the drama is, "Will Jeff be open to receiving love and support from the Clarks, or will he resist because he feels undeserving?" How willing are we to accept God's gracious gifts to us?

Cast:
>JEFF
>MRS. CLARK/JILL
>MR. CLARK/GARY

Props:
>2 chairs
>Small table
>Magazines
>Soft drink
>3 bags of groceries
>A large bag of barbecue briquettes
>Set of car keys

Setting: A family home

(There are two chairs and a small table with magazines. JEFF, a teenager, enters drinking a soft drink. JEFF is a foster child living with the Clarks. He plops down in one of the chairs, picks up a magazine, and leafs through it. JILL enters and starts across stage. She carries a bag of groceries on her way to "kitchen.")

JEFF: Hey, Mrs. Clark. Do you need some help with the groceries?

MRS. CLARK: Oh, thanks, Jeff, but I think Gary's bringing in the last two sacks. And really, it isn't necessary to call me "Mrs. Clark." I'd rather you call me Jill. *(Crosses offstage with groceries)*

(MR. CLARK/GARY enters carrying two bags of groceries.)

JEFF: Is that it, Mr. Clark? *(Jumps up to take sacks)*

GARY: That's it. (JEFF *takes groceries.*) Oh, thanks, Jeff.

JEFF (*begins to exit to kitchen, calls back to* GARY): So, what's for dinner?

GARY: I got some New York steaks—your favorite.

JEFF (*excited*): Aw-right!

GARY: We'll barbecue them to medium-rare perfection. I'll teach you all my tricks.

JEFF: That sounds great.

(JEFF *exits.* GARY *looks after him proudly.* JILL *enters from "kitchen."*)

JILL: Jeff's putting the rest of the food away. He's really a big help, you know.

GARY: Yeah, he's a great kid. I think this foster parent thing is working out really well. Jeff seems very happy here with us. (*Starts to sit*)

JILL: Yeah, I don't know what I was so worried about. Hey, before you get too comfortable, will you light the charcoal while I make a salad? I'd like to eat by six.

GARY: Oh, no. (JEFF *enters, listening.*) We forgot to buy charcoal! I used up the last of the briquettes on Saturday.

JILL (*disappointed*): Oh, well, I'll just broil the steaks or something. (*Points at* GARY) We have *got* to get a gas barbecue!

GARY: Yeah, well, then we'd just run out of propane.

JEFF: Hey, why don't I just run down to the store on my bike. That's no big deal. I can be back in 20 minutes or so.

GARY: Really? You wouldn't mind doing that?

JEFF: Oh no, Mr. Clark. That's well worth a barbecued steak dinner!

GARY: Well (*reaching into pocket, pulls out keys*), why don't you just take the car. (*Tosses keys to* JEFF. JILL *looks concerned.* GARY *starts to hand some money to* JEFF.) Here, buy a big bag. (*Pulls back money*) On one condition—that you stop calling us Mr. and Mrs. Clark and you start calling us Gary and Jill.

JEFF (*hesitantly*): Well, OK, Mr.—I mean, Gary. I don't know. I've always found it safer to call my foster parents Mister and Misses. That makes the break a little easier when I leave.

GARY: Well, there's no need to talk about leaving, Jeff. You're doing just fine here, don't you think? (*Looks toward* JILL *for reinforcement*) We're all doing just fine!

JEFF (*risking his feelings*): You guys have been great. This is definitely the best place I've ever stayed.

GARY: Well, good! Now, go get that charcoal. We've got some serious barbecuing to do.

(JEFF *exits excitedly, tossing keys in the air and catching them.* GARY *crosses to chair as* JILL *studies him.*)

JILL (*pausing*): So, you seem to be having a really good time with Jeff staying here.

GARY: Yes, dear. Yes, I am. I am having a marvelous time. That Jeff is quite a kid—quite a kid.

JILL: Yeah, he's great. It's going to be sad to see him leave when he gets a permanent home.

GARY: You know, Jill, I've been giving that some thought.

JILL: I knew it! Now, Gary, we agreed that this was a temporary situation.

GARY: Yeah, but that was before we got to know Jeff. He's doing so well with us. We can't let him go to another foster home. You heard him. We're the best family he's ever stayed with. Come on, Jill.

JILL (*warily*): What are you suggesting, Gary?

GARY: Look, Honey, I want us to adopt Jeff. Let's make him our son—legally. Let's give him our last name and our front door key. Let's make him our beneficiary; for better, for worse.

JILL: It's that "worse" part I'm worried about. You know, Jeff hasn't exactly lived a spotless existence. He's been in quite a lot of trouble in the past. And now you want to hand over the keys to the kingdom to him—just like that. I don't know, Gary.

GARY: He hasn't gotten into any trouble since he's been here.

JILL (*skeptically*): Not that we know of. Although you did just give him a wad of bills and your car keys. (*Pause*) Shouldn't he be back by now?

GARY: Well, what can you expect from a kid who doesn't even know who he is? The longest he's ever lived with one family is two years. He's got no foundation. He's never experienced the kind of love that can wipe out the dark places in his life. Maybe he's never experienced love at all. We can give him that. (*Pause*) We won't look at him as just a bad kid who needs help. We'll look at him as our son. A worthy person with endless possibilities for his life. That's how I see him, Jill. That's all I can see in him.

JILL (*pausing*): Well, I guess if that's all you see, that's what he must be.

GARY: Thanks, Honey. (*Hugging her*) I know we'll never regret this.

(JEFF *enters with a large bag of briquettes, sets it on floor.*)

JEFF: This was the biggest bag they had. Here's your change, Mr. . . . I mean, Gary.

GARY: Thanks, Jeff. Why don't you come over and sit down a minute. (*Cross to chairs*) Jill and I want to talk to you about a vision we have.

Curtain

I Love You More

Theme: How Vast Is the Love of Christ

Scripture: Ephesians 3:14-21

Synopsis: In Paul's letter to the Ephesians, he prays that they would be "rooted and established in love" and may have "power . . . to grasp how wide and long and high and deep is the love of Christ . . . love that surpasses knowledge." Love that is beyond what we can imagine. In "I Love You More," I have set up a situation where two people try to explain and compare the love they feel for each other. In their effort to outdo each other, they lose track of what it is they are talking about. As part of our spiritual discipline, I believe we need to continue to expand our acceptance and understanding of the love God and Christ offer to each of us. We are eager to limit ourselves, and yet we believe in a God who is limitless. What does God's limitless love mean for our lives?

Cast:
GERALD
KAREN

Props:
Park bench
Potted plants
Bouquet of flowers

Setting: A park setting

(There is a park bench at CS. A few potted plants around the bench to suggest a park. KAREN enters. She is dressed very nicely. She is taking a break from work to meet GERALD. KAREN looks around briefly, then sits on the bench. You may have a couple stroll along behind her or have a child and an adult walk by. KAREN looks around for GERALD. GERALD enters holding a bouquet of flowers. He sneaks up behind KAREN and speaks from behind the bench. GERALD and KAREN are hopelessly in love. This drama should be presented tongue-in-cheek. Age is not crucial to these characters.)

GERALD *(softly):* Boo!

KAREN *(startled, but delighted):* Oh, Gerald!

GERALD: Have you been waiting long?

KAREN: I just got here.

GERALD *(sits next to KAREN, hands her flowers):* These are for you.

KAREN: Oh, Gerald. They're beautiful. Thank you. You're the most thoughtful man alive.

GERALD: Well, after all, it is our anniversary.

KAREN: What are you talking about? We aren't getting married until next month.

GERALD: That is true. But it was eight months ago today that you first asked to borrow my stapler. And I knew right then and there that my days of searching were over. I erased all the phone numbers in my little, black database and devoted all my floppy disks to you and you alone.

KAREN: Oh, Gerald. You have such a way with words. You should have been a poet or a songwriter or something like that.

GERALD: Dear Karen, I was just an ordinary hacker until I met you. And now I have my own private muse of poetic inspiration.

KAREN: Well, I may not have your gift for words, but my affection for you is nevertheless as real. These flowers may be fragrant, but they cannot compare with the sweetness of your smile.

GERALD: And never has there been a sky true-bluer than your eyes.

KAREN: I know my love for you runs deeper than the deepest ocean.

GERALD: But can you compare your feelings to a mighty, rushing river coursing its way to the sea, as I can.

KAREN: A mighty, rushing river would be too sedate to illustrate my love for you. Perhaps my feelings are more akin to a hurricane-force wind, removing everything in its path just to get to your heart.

(Becoming competitive)

GERALD: Well, certainly that does sound extreme, my dear, but I might simply say that my love for you is as smooth and mellow as a fine, mature wine.

KAREN: What a lovely thought that is, and yet my love for you is more precious than the most valued work of art.

GERALD: Well, that truly may be, darling one, but have you called my name to every star in the heavens as I have done with yours?

KAREN: No, not the stars, but I have sung to the moon and heard your name echo back to me, for my love stretches throughout the darkness to pierce the night.

GERALD: I see. How poignant. *(Competition intensifies.* GERALD *stands and paces.)* OK. OK, but my love for you is as bright as the sun on a warm, summer day. It radiates from my face to each and every person I encounter just as the endless beams of solar light gently grace the cold, dark earth. Can you top that?

KAREN *(stands and paces as she thinks)*: Did I mention the hurricane already?

GERALD: Yes, we have covered hurricanes.

KAREN: What about mountains? Did I compare my love to mountains in any way?

GERALD: I don't think so.

KAREN *(victorious)*: OK, I get mountains!

GERALD *(challenging)*: Oh, yeah? Well, what about the mountains?

KAREN *(emphatically):* Oh, I don't know. My love for you is as tall as them or as wide as them or as old as them or something along those lines and because of that, I must love you more than you can even imagine. So there.

GERALD *(pausing):* You love me more than I can imagine?

KAREN: Definitely, more than you can even imagine!

GERALD *(pausing, stunned):* Wow. That's a lot.

KAREN: You bet it is, buddy.

(Both sit on bench)

GERALD *(simply):* Well, good. I love you too.

(GERALD rests his head on KAREN's shoulder, she rests her head on his head as they look out at congregation and smile contentedly.)

Curtain

The Greatest of These

Theme: Faith, Hope, and Love

Scripture: 1 Corinthians 13:1-13

Synopsis: Faith, hope, and love—but the greatest of these is love. Love is God present in our lives. Love is choosing to see life as God sees it. Love transforms, heals, forgives, and nourishes us. Love is the source of our very existence. In "The Greatest of These" I have set up a situation where the characters must choose between a response of love or a response of judgment. The grandmother's devotion to her grandchild is a witness for love. Do we choose to see love where it exists all around us, or are we tempted to see the negative side of events? We value faith, and we hope for each new dawning, but love is with us now and always. Love is who we are created to be.

Cast:
> ANGIE
> CAROL

Props:
> Dinette table
> 2 chairs
> Peanut butter sandwiches
> Bags of groceries
> Apples

Setting: A family dining room or kitchen

(There is a dinette table and at least two chairs. As the scene opens we see CAROL busy making peanut butter sandwiches. ANGIE enters laden with groceries. She calls back out the "door" to the imaginary children. During the scene, the two women can unpack groceries, make sandwiches, or do other business with the food items.)

ANGIE *(to children):* You kids stay in the backyard, OK? We'll call you when it's time to watch "Beauregard the Dinosaur." You still have a few minutes to play. *(To CAROL)* I brought chips and fruit. Do your kids like apples?

CAROL: Sure. Thanks. I hope your kids like peanut butter and jelly.

ANGIE: Oh, of course. It would be completely unkidlike not to like peanut butter. It's as natural for them as liking "Beauregard the Dinosaur." *(Sighing)* Now why couldn't I have thought of that? A television show for kids that stars a big, silly, green dinosaur named Beauregard singing and dancing and teaching helpful little lessons. Happy, happy, happy! *(Grumbling)* Why didn't I think of that? I could be retired by now and living it up in the sun somewhere.

CAROL: Oh, you're just too busy acting as chauffeur, cook, housecleaner, social director, and all-around mentor to the younger members of the neighborhood. You don't have time to think.

ANGIE: But, I heard that it was the mother of an overactive two-year-old who came up with the Beauregard idea. I think I need to expand my world a little. I just don't seem to do anything for myself these days. Too much kid duty.

CAROL: Well, it's funny, but I get a lot more done when your Katie is here entertaining Aaron. They sure are fast friends.

ANGIE: They sure are. Their preschool teacher told me that Katie and Aaron are inseparable. They sit together during story time, snack time, sharing time . . . and all those other "times" they have. Katie, Aaron, and . . . what's that other little boy's name?

CAROL: You mean Mark?

ANGIE: Yeah, that's right, Mark. He plays with them all the time. They're just like the Three Musketeers. It's so cute. *(Having a new thought)* Boy, I wish I had the child care setup that Mark's mother has. His grandmother, Mrs. Stewart, is with that little boy all the time. She takes him to preschool. She picks him up. She even takes a turn providing snacks and going on field trips. That is some great child care setup for Mark's mom. *(Pause. CAROL is noticeably silent.)* What's wrong? What'd I say?

CAROL: Well, I guess you don't know. Mark's grandmother isn't his baby-sitter, Carol. She has full custody of Mark.

ANGIE *(concerned):* No kidding? What happened to his parents? Did they die or something?

CAROL: No. I don't know anything about his father, but his mother isn't able to take care of him right now. She's in a treatment center upstate from here.

(Pause. CAROL uncomfortably anticipates response.)

CAROL: Don't even say it, Angie.

ANGIE *(innocently):* What? I didn't say anything!

CAROL: I know. But you're dying to make some little judgmental remark about parents being responsible for their own kids. Well, it isn't always that easy.

ANGIE *(with subtle sarcasm):* Easy? Whoever said it was easy? There's nothing easy about taking care of children.

CAROL: See. There you go. I knew you couldn't resist.

ANGIE: Oh, come on. You really think I'm so terrible? I just don't see what good it does to let Mark's mother off the hook. I mean, how is she ever going to learn to be responsible if someone else takes over for her.

CAROL: It's not a question of her *wanting* to take care of him. Mark's mother *can't* take care of him. The family has to think about what's best for Mark.

ANGIE: Well, how would you like to be saddled with a kid when you had finally earned some retirement. I love my kids, but I'm looking forward to having them grown up and on their own.

CAROL: Mrs. Stewart hopes beyond hope that her daughter will be able to be a loving, responsible parent again. She has faith that it is going to happen. But, in the meantime, Mark needs love. He needs a family. He needs security. He needs food on the table and clean clothes to wear, and that's the priority. I think she's a wonderful person to give so much of herself for Mark.

ANGIE *(pause):* Well, she does look pretty happy when she's with him.

CAROL: She sure does. I guess love works both ways—it's a gift to the giver and to the receiver.

ANGIE *(lifting the mood):* Oh well, as long as everyone's happy, who am I to judge? *(Crosses to "door," calls to children)* Kids, it's time to watch your favorite green dinosaur! *(To* CAROL*)* They love him—so, who am I to judge?

Curtain